ROUSING SONGS
& TRUE TALES OF THE
CIVIL WAR
BY
WAYNE ERBSEN

Tennessee State Museum

*"I only know two tunes; one is
'Yankee Doodle' and the other isn't."*
-General Ulysses S. Grant

Order No. NGB-950   ISBN:1-883206-33-2
©1999 by Native Ground Music, Inc.
International Copyright Secured. All Rights Reserved.

CONTENTS

N.C. Division of Archives & History

An old man in Georgia was asked which side he took in the conflict. *"I ain't took no side; but both side have took me!"*[28]

MUSIC OF THE CIVIL WAR

hen General Robert E. Lee said, "I don't believe we can have an army without music," he wasn't just "whistling 'Dixie.'" For soldiers in both armies, music played a vital role in uplifting morale, rallying patriotism, banishing loneliness, fighting homesickness and raising spirits. Music followed Civil War soldiers everywhere. They were awakened in the morning with the first call of the bugle, riveted into step by drums and fifes, serenaded in camp by banjos, fiddles and harmonicas, and even put to sleep by a lone bugler. But although instrumental music was linked to almost every step the soldier made, it was the songs that mattered most. Sung by both soldiers and by those who stayed behind, it was the songs that truly expressed the emotions, fired the patriotism and filled the emptiness felt by leaving loved ones at home and facing death at every turn.

As you thumb through *Rousing Songs & True Tales of the Civil War*, notice that the songs are arranged in alphabetical order, to aid you in finding them. The book is filled with many of the most popular songs of the war, along with the stories of how they were written. It includes both Confederate and Union songs, although the soldiers themselves often defied logic and sang songs of the other side, often without changing the words. As you sing these songs, you'll be transported to the eve of a battle

or to a parlor where wives and sweethearts await word of the fate of their soldiers. Either way, you'll feel both the joys and the sorrows of those who lived through the Civil War.

> *"General Jones...rides just like he has a boil on his stern."*
> Alabama soldier[40]

ithin three days of the firing on Fort Sumter, the first published song of the war was already on the streets. Entitled "The First Gun is Fired! May God Protect the Right!," it was written by George F. Root (1820-95) and published by Root & Cady.

With the coming of the war, publishers on both sides received an enormous economic boost. In 1861 alone, an estimated 2,000 pieces of music were written and published in both the North and the South. By the war's end, this figure had grown to some 10,000 songs. But for all the frenzy in music publishing, the war resulted in not only some of the best but also some of the worst music imaginable. For every composition that was even remotely popular, numerous "copycat" songs appeared. Songs were shamelessly pirated from the other side without the slightest twinge of remorse.

Songwriters, then known as "songsmiths," composed music to appeal to every conceivable emotion. They crafted patriotic and rallying songs, marching songs, comic or humorous songs and even rowdy drinking songs. Most popular were the deeply sentimental ballads that reminded both soldiers and the folks at home of the true costs of the war.

> *"I don't know what we would have done without our band."*
> **Soldier from 24th Massachusetts Regiment, April 1862**

SOUTHERN MUSIC PUBLISHING

efore the war, the South had relied mainly on the North for its supply of printed music. With the coming of secession, the South's few music publishers sprang into action. The first published song after South Carolina's secession was "The Palmetto State Song."[32]

Southern music publishers faced major obstacles in supplying the demand for printed music to the South. Their biggest challenge was in obtaining the necessary supplies of ink, paper and type, which had always been imported from the North. Some publishers, like J.C. Schreiner of Macon, resorted to smuggling a satchel of music type through Union lines in Tennessee. The soldiers apparently had not heard the oft quoted phrase from 1839, "The pen is mightier than the sword."

As the Northern blockade of Southern ports exerted a strangle hold on the South, the quality of printed music in the South sharply deteriorated. At the beginning of the war, Southern music was printed on heavy paper with dark black ink. By the war's end, music was printed on paper so thin that it collapsed when leaned against a music stand and the ink was so light that one had to strain to read it. Southern newspapers also suffered from the lack of paper and they often were forced to use paper made of straw, cornhusks and cotton. Some even printed editions of their newspaper on the blank sides of wallpaper.[32] Although the quality of Confederate printed music declined as the years wore on, its impact on the morale of Southern people was as potent as ever. In contrast, Northern presses enjoyed abundant quantities of needed materials, and the quality of their work remained high throughout the war.[2]

Sovereignty Flag of South Carolina

"The South must not only fight her own battles, but must sing her own songs." The J. Black Company, Mobile, Alabama, 1861

PRINTED MUSIC

ome of the earliest songs of the war were produced as single sheets known as "broadsides." Often sold on the streets by young boys, they functioned almost like a newspaper. Because they seldom included musical notation, broadsides could be produced quickly, often appearing on the streets within hours of a battle or a newsworthy event. Music was also commonly published as sheet music. The front cover of the sheet music was usually ornately illustrated with the title and the name of the composer emblazoned on the front in highly decorated typeface. Most sheet music consisted of one large sheet of paper folded in the middle with an extra sheet sandwiched in the middle. The second and sixth pages were often left blank.

For the soldiers themselves, publishers produced small pocket songbooks known as "songsters." Printed without music, they contained only the words to the best known songs, often without attributing the songs to a particular composer. Besides the Bible, these pocket songsters were the books most commonly carried by Civil War soldiers, North and South. As one Confederate soldier wrote in his diary, "We kept song books with us and passed much of our leisure time singing. I carried my book even through prison and brought it home with me."[9]

My Colonel is "an ignoramus fit for nothing higher than *the cultivation of corn.*" *Rebel soldier*

THE MILITARY BANDS

lmost oblivious to the struggles and successes of music publishers in the big cities far away were the Union and Confederate soldiers themselves. To them, music meant relief from boredom and stress and a way to kindle memories of loved ones and home. Many soldiers relished performances by the regimental bands, which were far more prevalent in the North than in the South. A performance by a military band often included marches, patriotic songs, old favorites, religious melodies, dance tunes, classical music and popular songs of the day.[35]

Although military bands were normally moved out of harm's way before a battle, in several instances they were ordered to "strike up the band" in the heat of battle. Union General Sheridan ordered his military band to the front at the battle of Dinwiddie Court House and ordered them to play loudly their gayest tunes and "never mind if a bullet goes through a trombone or even a trombonist, now and then."[31] In response, a Confederate band was brought to the front to counteract the fervor generated by the Federal band. A first-hand account of "battle of the bands" was later written by the commander of the 1st Maine Cavalry:

"Our band came up from the rear and cheered and animated our hearts by its rich music; ere long a Rebel band replied by giving us Southern airs; with cheers from each side in encouragement of its own band, a cross-fire of "The Star Spangled Banner," "Yankee Doodle" and "John Brown" mingled with "Dixie" and "Bonnie Blue Flag."[31]

MUSIC OF THE COMMON SOLDIERS

s popular as the regimental bands were to Civil War soldiers, the music enjoyed most by soldiers on both sides was the music made by their fellow soldiers. Lucky was a camp that could boast a banjo player, a fiddler or even a good harmonica or jew's harp player. Tunes often played by Confederate musicians included "Arkansas Traveler," "The Goose Hangs High," "Billy in the Low Grounds," "Money Musk," and "Hell Broke Loose in Georgia." Such tunes were favored by fiddlers on both sides who played for soldier dances like the cotillion and the Virginia Reel. In place of female dance partners, soldiers often tied a handkerchief or rag around the left arm to denote a woman.[28]

Although soldiers enjoyed instrumental music, by far the most common musical outlet was singing. Soldiers sang, whistled and hummed on marches, behind earthworks, while waiting for orders, in camp and even on the eve of a battle, with their muskets primed and ready. They sang solo, in duets, trios, and they often formed glee clubs. Sometimes entire regiments, Generals and all, sang on marches. Some soldiers paid with their lives when their song tipped off their location to a enemy sharpshooter.

T. Scott Sanders

"Bang, bang, bang, a rattle, de bang, bang, bang, a boom, de bang...whirr-siz-siz-siz - a ripping, roaring, boom, bang!"
Sam Watkins, Confederate Private describing a "fire fight."[7]

MUSIC OF THE COMMON SOLDIERS

Texas State Library

To many soldiers, the favorite place to sing was in the evening around the campfire. For both armies, the best-loved songs were often the old favorites which had been nationally popular long before the war.

Although music certainly fanned the flames of patriotic zeal, for soldiers on both sides it occasionally served to remind them of their common heritage. On the eve of the final day of battle at Murfreesboro, on July 1, 1863, Union and Confederate bands took turns playing tunes for their men. Finally, when one band struck up "Home! Sweet Home!" both bands, and most of the soldiers on both sides joined in.[10] On another occasion, a Confederate soldier

named Goodwin was being baptized in the Rapidan River in northern Virginia. A group of passing Union soldiers heard the hymn singing and joined in singing "There is a Fountain Filled With Blood."

For many soldiers, who had never traveled more than twenty miles from home, the Civil War changed their musical tastes forever. For the first time, many were exposed to instruments like the banjo, the harmonica and the jew's harp. By mixing with soldiers from other regions of the country, they learned new songs and became acquainted with musical styles they had never heard before. The memory of these new sounds lingered long after the din of battle had faded away.

"Our Congress are a set of blockheads."
Isaac Alexander, Confederate soldier, February 21, 1864[7]

SOLDIER HUMOR

No Fleas on Him!

A soldier in the 25th Maine was scratching himself with both hands when an officer who was passing by inquired, "What's the matter, my man, fleas?" "Fleas!" said the soldier in a tone of utter contempt. "Do you think I am a dog? Them is lice."[39]

Hindquarters

After President Lincoln named General Hooker to take over the army, the President received word that the General was sending out dispatches from his "headquarters in the saddle." Grinning to an aide, Lincoln said, *"The trouble with Hooker is that he's got his headquarters where his hindquarters ought to be."*[42]

Herb Peck, Jr.

A soldier made the mistake of getting too close to the rear end of a mule. His companions caught him on the fly, placed him on a stretcher and headed for a makeshift hospital. On the way, the soldier came to. He gazed at the sky overhead and felt the swaying motion of the stretcher. Feebly, he lowered his hand over the side to find nothing but air. "My God," he groaned, "I haven't even hit the ground yet!"

"It takes one half of the men to keep the other half from running away." **James Bracy, Confederate soldier. May 11, 1863.**[7]

While fighting on the Rappahannock, General Early saw a chaplain running away from the scene of the battle. To the chaplain the General said, "For twenty years you have been wanting to get to heaven, and now that there is a chance, you run away from it!"

"I wish you could hear a [soldier] of the 1st Texas Calvary sing. His song is a cross between the bray of a jackass and the note of a turkey buzzard, and far excels either in melody." A soldier stationed at Baton Rouge[28]

An arithmetic book published in the South during the war included this problem, "If one Confederate soldier can whip 7 Yankees, how many Confederate soldiers can whip 49 Yankees?"[10]

After a dog tried to steal his food, one soldier said, "I say, Jim, look out there! That dog is after your rations!" "Never mind," said Jim. "I'll bet five dollars he can't eat 'em!"[39]

One Connecticut soldier claimed that his company had eaten so much mule meat that the ears of every man had grown 3 1/2 inches.[39]

One story tells that on "Stonewall" Jackson's death, several angels came down to escort him to heaven only to find that he had beaten them to it by making a rapid flank march.[10]

General "Stonewall" Jackson

"Uncal Sam has as much care for his Nefews as he has for one of his mules or horses." Union soldier

Treason!

After President Lincoln dismissed General McClellan, Septimus Winner composed a song entitled "Give Us Back Our Old Commander." Winner soon found himself accused of treason. After promising to stop publication of the song, charges were dismissed. Winner does have the distinction of being America's only songwriter to be charged with treason for writing a song.

"Go boys, to your country's call! I'd rather be a brave man's widow than a coward's wife." Chanted by the women of Eucheeanna, Florida as they marched through town, early 1861.[7]

A gentleman who called upon Lincoln to request a pass through the lines to Richmond was told, "Well, I would be very happy to oblige you, if my passes were respected; but the fact is, sir, I have, within the last two years, given passes to 250,000 men to go to Richmond, and not one has got there yet."[10]

ALL QUIET ALONG THE POTOMAC TONIGHT

While soldiers were fighting in the fields and valleys, another battle raged over the authorship of one of the best-loved songs of the Civil War, "All Quiet Along the Potomac Tonight." On November 30, 1861, a poem entitled "The Picket Guard" was anonymously published in *Harper's Weekly*. Among those who claimed credit for writing it were Thaddeus Oliver of Georgia, and Lamar Fontaine of Mississippi. Of the two, Fontaine was the most tenacious in claiming authorship. As a Major with the Second Virginia Cavalry, he claimed he was inspired to write the poem after visiting a friend on picket duty. When the soldier stirred the coals of his campfire, a Union sharpshooter on the opposite bank noticed his position and shot him. As he tried to give comfort to his dying friend, his eyes fell on the headlines of a newspaper that was lying nearby, "All Quiet Along the Potomac." Although this gripping account makes for fascinating reading, it was most probably pulp fiction.

The real author of "The Picket Guard" was undoubtedly Mrs. Ethel Lynn Eliot Beers of Goshen, New York. Her inspiration to write the poem came not on the battlefield but by reading newspaper accounts of the war.

"The Picket Guard" became immediately popular on both sides of the conflict. In the North, the poem was set to music by at least four different composers, including H. Coyle, W.H. Goodwin, J. Dayton and David A. Warden. In the South, it was John Hill Hewitt (1801-90) who composed the music for the poem in 1864. It is Hewitt's melody that is most commonly sung.

An English officer visiting Texas wrote of hearing a Confederate band "braying discordantly" while another Britisher said that bands were "wretched" and their "dismal noises an intolerable nuisance."[28]

ALL QUIET ALONG THE POTOMAC TONIGHT

"All qui - et a - long the Po - to - mac to - night," Ex -
cept here and there a stray pick - et Is shot as he walks on his
beat to and fro By a ri - fle - man hid in the thick - et; 'Tis
noth - ing! a pri - vate or two now and then Will not count in the news of the
bat - tle; Not an of - fi - cer lost! on - ly one of the men Moan - ing
out, all a - lone, the death rat - tle. "All qui - et a -
long the Po - to - mac to - night!"

Just after the first Battle of Bull Run a newsboy with an armload of papers was shouting *"Extra! Extra! All About the Battle."* An officer purchased a copy but quickly complained to the newsboy that "I don't see any battle in this paper." *"Don't you?"* said the boy. *"Well, you won't see any battle if you loaf around this hotel all the time"*[28]

"Farwell Gould rode into battle at Pea Ridge with a jug of whiskey in his hand because there wasn't a safe place to sit it down." Vance Randolph

ALL QUIET ALONG THE POTOMAC TONIGHT

"All quiet along the Potomac tonight,"
Where soldiers lie peacefully dreaming,
And their tents in the rays of the clear autumn moon,
And the light of the campfires are gleaming;
There's only the sound of the lone sentry's tread,
As he tramps from the rock to the fountain,
And thinks of the two on the low trundle bed
Far away in the cot on the mountain.

His musket falls slack-his face, dark and grim,
Grows gentle with memories tender,
As he mutters a prayer for the children asleep,
And their mother - "May heaven defend her!"
The moon seems to shine as brightly as then-
That night, when the love yet unspoken
Leaped up to his lips, and when low murmured vows
Were pledged to be ever unbroken.

Then drawing his sleeve roughly o'er his eyes,
He dashes off the tears that are welling;
And gathers his gun close up to his breast,
As if to keep down the heart's swelling.
He passes the fountain, the blasted pine tree,
And his footstep is lagging and weary,
Yet onward he goes, thro' the broad belt of light,
Toward the shades of the forest so dreary.

Hark! was it the night-wind that rustles the leaves!"
Was it the moonlight so wond'rously flashing?
It look'd like a rifle! "Ah, Mary, good bye!"
As his life-blood is ebbing and plashing.
"All quiet along the Potomac to-night,"
No sound save the rush of the river;
While soft falls the dew on the face of the dead,
"The Picket's" off duty for ever.

> *"I would as soon kiss a dried codfish as one of them."*
> A Union soldier referring to Southern women

THE BATTLE CRY OF FREEDOM

erhaps no other Union song fired up the flames of patriotism among both soldiers and civilians as "The Battle Cry of Freedom." Its effect was so electric that it was sung not only at war rallies all across the North, but several Union Generals ordered their men to sing it while charging headlong into battle.

Needing a song to compete with "The Battle Cry of Freedom," Confederate song writers composed several sets of lyrics to the original melody.

Published in 1862 by Root & Cady, the words and music of "The Battle Cry of Freedom" were composed by George F. Root. He wrote it on May 3, 1861 after hearing of President Lincoln's proclamation that the army and navy would be increased by 175,000 men. We are fortunate to have Root's own account of composing it: "I heard of President Lincoln's second call for troops one afternoon while reclining on a lounge in my brother's house. I thought it out that afternoon, and wrote it the next morning at the store."[16] The "store" was Root's second story office at the publishing house of Root & Cady in Chicago.

Hardly had the ink dried on his new song, when the Lumford Brothers appeared at Root's door. They came looking for a new song to sing at a huge patriotic rally to be held just opposite Root & Cady's office building in the courthouse square. So within minutes after learning Root's new song, the Lumford Brothers were singing it to the uproarious approval of the crowd, who joined them in a rousing

George F. Root

version of the chorus. The song quickly spread throughout the Northern states.

THE BATTLE CRY OF FREEDOM

O n August 2, 1862 the *Chicago Daily Tribune* reported that "no meeting was complete without 'The Battle Cry of Freedom.'" One of the reasons it was so quickly established as the preeminent patriotic song of the Union was that at the time it was published, Root & Cady was the most successful publishing company in America. As such, they were in a perfect position to promote and distribute it through their publishing network. The song was so successful, in fact, that fourteen printing presses could not meet the demand. Between 500,000 and 700,000 copies of "The Battle Cry of Freedom" were printed.[6]

The power of "The Battle Cry of Freedom" to evoke feelings of patriotic fervor are revealed in many published testimonials: "It was a nasty night during the Seven Days fight when some fellow on the other side struck up that song and others joined in on the chorus until it seemed to me the whole Yankee army was singing. A man with me said, 'Good heavens, Cap, what are those fellows made of anyway? Here we've licked them six days running and now on the eve of the seventh they're singing 'Rally Round the Flag!' I am not normally superstitious, but I tell you that song sounded to me like the 'death

knell' and my heart went down into my boots; and though I've tried to do my duty, it has been an uphill fight with me ever since that night." Confederate officer just after General Lee's surrender in April 1865.[5]

A Union veteran later recalled when a glee club from Chicago sang a new song, "The Battle Cry of Freedom" after the battle of Stone's River at Murfreesboro, Tennessee.

"We are between a sh-t and a sweat out here."
Federal soldier in a letter to his wife.[40]

"The effect was little short of miraculous. It put as much spirit and cheer into the army as a victory. Day and night one could hear it by every camp fire and in every tent. I never shall forget how the men rolled out the line, "And although he may be poor, he shall never be a slave."[23]

Charles A. Dana, editor of the *New York Sun* said in October, 1897 that "Dr. Root did more to preserve the Union than a great many brigadier-generals, and quite as much as some brigades."

In his 1891 autobiography, George F. Root wrote,

"The song went into the army, and the testimony in regard to its use in the camp and on the march, and even on the field of battle, from soldiers and officers, up to generals, and even to the good President himself, made me thankful that if I could not shoulder a musket in defense of my country I could serve her in this way."[16]

U.S. Army Military History Institute

Trying to keep hungry soldiers from foraging was as easy as waltzing with a grizzly bear. One Federal soldier was stopped on his way into camp with a fine goose hung over his shoulder. Questioned where he got it, he said, "*I was coming through the village whistling 'Yankee Doodle' and this confounded Rebel of a goose came out and hissed me; so I shot it.*"[28]

THE BATTLE CRY OF FREEDOM

Yes, we'll ral-ly 'round the flag, boys, we'll ral-ly once a-gain, Shout-ing the bat-tle cry of Free-dom, We will ral-ly from the hill-side, we'll gath-er from the plain, Shout-ing the bat-tle cry of Free-dom. The

Chorus

Un-ion for-ev-er, Hur-rah! boys, hur-rah! Down with the trait-or, up with the star, While we ral-ly 'round the flag, boys, ral-ly once a-gain, Shout-ing the bat-tle cry of Free-dom.

We are springing to the call of our brothers gone before,
Shouting the battle cry of Freedom,
And we'll fill the vacant ranks with a million freemen more,
Shouting the battle cry of Freedom. (Chorus)

We will welcome to our numbers the loyal, true and brave,
Shouting the battle cry of Freedom,
And although they may be poor, not a man shall be a slave,
Shouting the battle cry of Freedom. (Chorus)

So we're springing to the call from the East and from the West,
Shouting the battle cry of Freedom,
And we'll hurl the rebel crew from the land we love the best,
Shouting the battle cry of Freedom. (Chorus)

A little Southern boy was walking by a group of Federal soldiers who were occupying Canton, Mississippi in 1864. After passing them he turned and shouted, *"Hurrah for Jeff Davis!"* One of the soldiers quickly responded with, *"Hurray for the devil."* *"That's right,"* said the boy. *"You hurrah for your Captain, and I'll hurrah for mine."*[39]

BATTLE HYMN OF THE REPUBLIC

ometime before 1855, William Steffe of South Carolina composed a Methodist camp meeting hymn entitled "Say, Brothers, Will You Meet Us." As a joke, the glee club of the Second Battalion, Massachusetts Volunteer Militia used this melody for a parody on Sergeant John Brown, the second tenor. As word of the song got out, the singing soldiers were surprised when it was widely assumed that the John Brown of the song was the infamous Kansas abolitionist.

With an infectious rhythm and an easy chorus, the popularity of the song quickly spread. Among the first to sing it was Colonel Fletcher Webster's 12th Massachusetts Regiment. On their way to the front in northern Virginia, they sang it with gusto as they marched through the streets of New York City on July 24, 1861. The crowd's wild and enthusiastic response earned Webster's soldiers the nickname, "The Hallelujah Regiment." The song became so popular, in fact, that it quickly became the marching song of the entire Union army. As the spirit of abolitionism took hold in the North, it was sung at every political rally and fund-raising meeting where it was known as "The John Brown Song," "John Brown's Body" or "Glory Hallelujah!"

While visiting a Union army outpost in northern Virginia in November, 1861, the song was heard by a group that included Julia Ward (Mrs. Samuel) Howe and Rev. James F. Clarke. A friend of the poet Longfellow, Mrs. Howe was herself a noted poetess who later gained fame as a champion of woman's suffrage and a proponent of Mother's Day.[25] On their return trip to Washington, Rev. Clark suggested to Mrs. Howe that she write a more dignified set of words to "John Brown's Body." In the early morning hours of the following day Mrs. Howe awoke in her room in the Willard Hotel, lit a candle, and "searched for an old sheet of paper and an old stump of a pen which I had had the night before, and began to scrawl the lines almost without looking...Having completed this, I lay down again and fell asleep, but not without feeling that something of importance had happened to me."[1]

BATTLE HYMN OF THE REPUBLIC

The poem composed by Mrs. Howe was submitted to the *Atlantic Monthly* and published anonymously on the front page of the February, 1862 issue. The title was supplied by the editor, James T. Fields, and the song was published by Oliver Ditson & Co. in 1862.

I have seen Him in the watch-fires of a hundred circling camps,
They have builded Him an altar in the evening dews and damps,
I can read His righteous sentence by the dim and flaring lamps:
His day is marching on. (Chorus)

I have read a fiery gospel writ in burnished rows of steel:
"As ye deal with my contemners, so with you my grace shall deal;
Let the Hero born of woman crush the serpent with his heel,
Since God is marching on. (Chorus)

He has sounded forth the trumpet that shall never call retreat;
He is sifting out the hearts of men before His judgment seat:
Oh, be swift, my soul, to answer Him! be jubilant, my feet!
Our God is marching on. (Chorus)

In the beauty of the lilies Christ was born across the sea,
With a glory in his bosom that transfigures you and me;
As he died to make men holy, let us die to make men free,
While God is marching on. (Chorus)

JOHN BROWN'S BODY

John Brown's body lies a-mouldering in the grave,
John Brown's body lies a-mouldering in the grave,
John Brown's body lies a-mouldering in the grave,
But his soul goes marching on.

Glory, glory, Hallelujah,
Glory, glory, Hallelujah,
Glory, glory, Hallelujah,
His soul goes marching on.

He's gone to be a soldier in the Army of the Lord,
His soul goes marching on. (Chorus)

John Brown's knapsack is strapped upon his back,
His soul goes marching on. (Chorus)

John Brown died that the slaves might be free,
But his soul goes marching on. (Chorus)

The stars above in Heaven now are looking kindly down,
On the grave of old John Brown. (Chorus)

John Brown

Herb Peck, Jr.

A young man was standing in line at a recruiting station when the man in front of him was released because one leg was shorter than the other. He protested that he had "both legs too short," but was signed up anyway.[29]

A soldier was telling his mother of the terrible fire at Chickamauga. "Why didn't you get behind a tree?" she asked. "Tree?" he said. "There wasn't enough for the officers![4]

During the battle of Kingston in 1864, a soldier was asked by a chaplain if he was supported by Divine Providence. *"No, we're supported by the 9th New Jersey."[39]*

THE BONNIE BLUE FLAG

To Albert Pike Esq., the Poet-Lawyer of Arkansas

After Dixie, the most popular song of the Confederacy was "The Bonnie Blue Flag." On January 9, 1861 a stage performer by the name of Harry Macarthy was in Jackson, Mississippi when the Convention of the People of Mississippi followed South Carolina's lead and adopted an Ordinance of Secession. Although born in England in 1834, Macarthy billed himself as "The Arkansas Comedian." A professional entertainer, he often appeared on stage decked out in a costume with a low-set collar, ruffled shirt front, wide wristbands and diamond rings on his fingers.

After Mississippi's Ordinance of Secession was signed, a blue flag with a white star was raised over the capital building in Jackson. Soon after witnessing this event, Macarthy was inspired to write the lyrics to "The Bonnie Blue Flag." For the melody, he borrowed the familiar Irish tune, "The Irish Jaunting Car."

It is unclear whether Macarthy completed the song in time to perform it at the end of Mississippi's secessionist convention. There is evidence that his sister, Marion Macarthy, sang it at the Variety Theatre in New Orleans and that Harry performed it in September, 1861 during one of his so-called "Personation Concerts" held at the New Orleans Academy of Music. The audience was filled with soldiers from Louisiana and Texas who were on their way to Virginia and the song received an overwhelming response. By then it was published by A.E. Blackmar & Bro. of 74 Camp St., New Orleans, who eventually issued it in six different editions. It was also printed in England, and several Northern publishers issued parodies of the song.

> "I want to be in one battle, just for the curiosity of the thing."
> George M. Decherd, Confederate soldier, January 6, 1862.[7]

THE BONNIE BLUE FLAG

Macarthy went on to sing "The Bonnie Blue Flag" in all the major cities of the South. His active concert schedule at the very time Southern patriotism was at fever pitch certainly helped to spread its popularity. In 1904, one old soldier wrote, "Often I have heard him sing it when thousands of people went wild with excitement and enthusiasm."[15]

General Benjamin Butler

"The Bonnie Blue Flag" was so popular that when New Orleans was occupied by Federal troops on April 28, 1862, Major General Benjamin Butler had the song's publisher, A.E. Blackmar, arrested and fined $500. Butler had all copies of the song destroyed and threatened to slap a $25 fine on any man, woman or child that sang, played or even whistled "The Bonnie Blue Flag."[2]

It is interesting to examine the third verse, which was apparently added after February 1, 1861, when all these states had seceded. Whoever wrote it erred in the order of secession. After South Carolina voted to secede December 20, 1860, the actual order of secession was Mississippi, Florida, Alabama, Georgia, Louisiana and Texas.[24]

> **First, gallant South Carolina nobly made the stand;**
> **Then came Alabama, who took her by the hand;**
> **Next, quickly, Mississippi, Georgia and Florida,**
> **All raised on high the Bonnie Blue flag that bears a Single Star.**

Though Macarthy's political sympathies lay with the Confederacy, he steadfastly avoided conscription by claiming British citizenship. When the Southern cause seemed to be lost, Macarthy fled to Philadelphia in 1864, never again to return to the South. After the war, he composed a parody on "The Bonnie Blue Flag," which seemed to praise reconciliation. He died in Oakland, California in 1888.

"Git thar fustest with the mostest." General Nathan Bedford Forrest, CSA

THE BONNIE BLUE FLAG

We are a band of bro-thers, and na-tive to the soil, Fight-ing for our pro-per-ty we gained by hon-est toil; And when our rights were threat-ened, the cry rose near and far, Hur-rah for the Bon-nie Blue Flag that bears a Sin-gle Star!

Chorus
Hur-ray! Hur-rah! for South-ern rights Hur-rah! Hur-rah for the Bon-nie Blue flag that bears a Sin-gle Star!

Every Last Chicken

An old lady complained to General O.H. Payne in 1865 that his soldiers had stolen every last chicken she had, and she demanded compensation. Trying to be as tactful as possible, the General apologized but added, *"Madam, we are determined to squelch out the rebellion if it costs every damned chicken in Tennessee."* [39]

Herb Peck, Jr.

"I reckon I killed as many of them as they did of me."
A wounded Confederate soldier. [28]

THE BONNIE BLUE FLAG

"It is well that war is so terrible, or we should grow too fond of it."
General Robert E. Lee, December 1862

We are a band of brothers, and native to the soil,
Fighting for our the property we gained by honest toil;
And when our rights were threatened, the cry rose near and far,
Hurrah for the Bonnie Blue Flag that bears a Single Star!

As long as the Union was faithful to her trust,
Like friends and like brethren, kind were we, and just;
But now, when Northern treachery attempts our rights to mar,
We hoise on high the Bonnie Blue Flag that bears a Single Star.

First, gallant South Carolina nobly made the stand;
Then came Alabama, who took her by the hand;
Next, quickly, Mississippi, Georgia and Florida,
All raised on high the Bonnie Blue flag that bears a Single Star.

Ye men of valor, gather round the Banner of the Right,
Texas and fair Louisiana, join us in the fight;
Davis, our loved President, and Stephens, statesmen rare,
Now rally round the Bonnie Blue Flag that bears a Single star.

And here's to brave Virginia! the Old Dominion State
With the young Confederacy at length has linked her fate;
Impelled by her example, now other States prepare
To hoist on high the Bonnie Blue Flag that bears a Single Star.

Then cheer, boys, cheer, raise the joyous shout,
For Arkansas and North Carolina now have both gone out;
And let another rousing cheer for Tennessee be given-
The Single Star of the Bonnie Blue Flag has grown to be Eleven.

Then here's to our Confederacy, strong we are and brave;
Like patriots of old, we'll fight our heritage to save;
And rather than submit to shame, to die we would prefer;
So, cheer for the Bonnie Blue Flag, that bears a Single Star.

While having supper with his staff at a hotel in Tennessee, General Rosecrans had the unfortunate experience of tasting the butter, which was old and rancid. He immediately shot out of his seat, stood at full attention, and gave the butter a snappy salute. *"Gentlemen,"* he explained, *"that butter outranks me!"*[39]

DIXIE'S LAND

"If I had known it was going to be so popular, I would have written it better." Daniel D. Emmett

They don't whistle "Dixie" much anymore. Even the name of Daniel D. Emmett, who composed it, is nearly forgotten. But travel back to early 1843 to a run-down boarding house on Catherine Street, in New York City. This was the home of Dan Emmett, who moved there from his native Ohio. After serving in the army as a drummer and fifer, he performed with the Cincinnati Circus Company, playing banjo and fiddle. His father had been an abolitionist and an early organizer of the underground railroad.

Advertising himself as "The Great Southern Banjo Melodiest" and "The Renowned Ethiopian Minstrel," Emmett performed in blackface with dancer Dick Pelham. Emmett also played with Billy Whitlock, who had studied banjo with Joel W. Sweeney, the man who claimed he added the 5th string to the banjo. While Emmett and Whitlock were practicing at Emmett's boarding house, they were paid an unexpected visit by Frank Brower, who joined them on bones and by Dick Pelham who played the tambourine. This was perhaps the first time all these instruments had played together in this combination. The excited musicians, who would soon be calling themselves "The Virginia Minstrels," then made the rounds of the "Branch" in the Bowery, and Bartlett's Billiard Room, where they were met with overwhelming, if intoxicated, response. The first minstrel band was born.

The country must have been ready. How else do you explain the sudden craze of minstrel music that swept the country, North, South, East and West? Minstrel bands were formed in most major American cities and traveling black-faced minstrel bands toured the country playing everywhere from the gold fields of California to the grand river boats traveling down the Mississippi River. The popularity of minstrel music was so great that some bands performed regularly in a single theater for as long as ten years!

General Pickett ordered "Dixie" played at a charge at Gettysburg.[35]

t the center of the raging popularity of minstrel music was Dan Emmett. Not only was he an active performer in New York, but he also took England by storm and returned to play with Bryant's Minstrels for a decade. Late one Saturday night, September 17, 1859, Emmett was paid a visit by Dan and Jerry Bryant, of Bryant's Minstrels. They asked Emmett to compose a snappy new walk-around to liven up their performance the following Monday night. In later years Emmett gave conflicting accounts of how he came to compose "Dixie."

"...I tried to think out something suitable, but my thinking apparatus was dormant; rather than disappoint Bryant, I searched through my trunk and resurrected the manuscript of "I Wish I Was in Dixie's Land," which I had written years before. I changed the tune and rewrote the verses, and in all likelihood, if Dan Bryant had not made that hurry-up request, "Dixie" never would have been brought out."[26]

Yet in another story of the origin of "Dixie," Emmett was unable to compose a new song on September 18, 1859, which was gloomy and rainy. He remarked to his wife, "I wish I was in Dixie, way down in the sunny South... I'd swap all of New York City for another day in Dixie." This, according to the story, provided the inspiration to complete the song. In less than an hour he composed the first verse and chorus.[27]

The house was packed the following Monday night, September 19, 1859, when Dan Emmett stepped on the stage at Mechanics' Hall to perform his new walk-around, "Dixie's Land." There was no mistaking it; the crowd went simply wild. One of America's greatest songs was getting its due.

DIXIE'S LAND

To Emmett, "Dixie" was probably just another song along the lines of the ones he had already composed: "Old Dan Tucker," (ca. 1845) and "The Blue Tailed Fly" (1846). Grabbing what he thought was a great offer, he sold all rights to the song for $300 to Firth, Pond and Co. who first published it on June 21, 1860.

The timing was nearly perfect. With the secession of the Southern states, an anthem was needed to fan the flames of Southern patriotism. As preparations were being made for the formal inauguration of Jefferson Davis as President of the Confederacy on February 22, 1862, the duty fell to Herman Arnold to select and arrange the music. By then, Dan Emmett's "Dixie's Land" was well-known as played by most minstrel bands then touring the South. Arnold's choice of "Dixie" was only natural. Not only was it the South's most popular song at that time, but the words also struck a responsive chord. After all, the seceding states did consider themselves to be a land apart, willing to "live and die in 'Dixie's Land.'" Although never officially declared, "Dixie" was certainly the Confederacy's most popular patriotic song and its unofficial national anthem.

After Lee's surrender, President Lincoln ordered the band to play "Dixie."
"I had always thought 'Dixie' one of the best tunes I have ever heard. Our adversaries over the way attempted to appropriate it, but I insisted yesterday that we fairly captured it. I presumed the opinion to the Attorney General, and he gave it as his legal opinion that it is our lawful prize. I now request the band to favor me with its performance."[26]
President Abraham Lincoln

DIXIE'S LAND

I wish I was in de land ob cot-ton, Old times dar am not for-got-ton, Look a - way! Look a - way! Look a - way! Dix-ie Land. In Dix-ie Land whar I was born in, Ear-ly on oge fros-ty morn-in', Look a - way! Look a - way! Look a - way! Dix-ie Land. Den I

Chorus

wish I was in Dix-ie, Hor - ray! Hor - ray! In Dix-ie Land I'll take my stand, To lib and die in Dix-ie, A - way, A - way, A - way down south in Dix-ie, A - way, A - way, A - way down south in Dix-ie.

"When a Southerner comes home with calloused hands, he's either been plowing or applauding 'Dixie.'" Old saying.

Ole missus marry "Will de weaver,"
Willium was a gay deceaber;
Look away, etc.
But when he put his arm around 'er,
He smiled as fierce as a forty pounder,
Look away, etc.

His face was sharp as a butcher's cleaber,
But dat did not seem to greab 'er;
Look away, etc.
Old missus acted de foolish part,
And died for a man dat broke her heart,
Look away, etc.

Now here's a health to the next old Misses,
An' all de gals dat want to kiss us;
Look away, etc.
But if you want to drive 'way sorrow,
Come and hear dis song tomorrow,
Look away, etc.

Dar's buckwheat cakes and Injun batter,
Makes you fat or a little fatter;
Look away, etc.
Den hoe it down an' scratch your grabble,
To Dixie's Land I'm bound to trabble,
Look away, etc.

"If I had known to what use they were going to put my song, I will be damned if I'd have written it!" Dan Emmett, after hearing the Confederates had adopted "Dixie" as their rallying cry.[14]

"Come on! Come on! Do you want to live forever?"
Unknown Confederate Colonel

THE FADED COAT OF BLUE

espite the clear-cut image of the "Blue and Gray," Civil War uniforms did not fall into two neat categories. Nearly every conceivable color and kind of uniform was worn by soldiers on both sides. In the early days of the war, gray uniforms were almost as common on Union soldiers as they were on Confederates.[13] In fact, many soldiers did without uniforms at all. To protest the lack of uniforms for a parade held in August, 1861, Company A of the 10th New York formed ranks wearing only white shirts and drawers![28]

Near the close of the war, J.H. McNaughton wrote the words and music to the heart-felt song, "The Faded Coat of Blue; or, The Nameless Grave." Though its original melody was soon forgotten, its lyrics were kept alive by those who cherished sentimental songs. Rural Southern musicians, who had a particular fondness for this type of song, often sang the words to a number of different melodies. Early recordings of the song, each with its own melody, included those by Owen Mills and Frank Welling, Buell Kazee and Maybelle Carter. The version recorded here is from the 1909 book, *Heart Songs*.

Other Civil War "jacket" songs included, "The Faded Gray Jacket; or, Fold It Up Carefully" (words by Mrs. C.A. Ball, music by Charlie Ward) and "The Coat of Faded Gray" (words by G.W. Harris, Music by H.M. Hall.)[2]

The Night the Bandmaster Got Drunk
The bandmaster of the 19th Virginia felt his services were not fully appreciated by the regimental Commander. One night, while on a blind drunk, the band leader stuck his head in the Colonel's tent and, at the top of his lungs, cried out, *"You are a damned old louse!"* When the band master awoke the next morning, he found himself in the guardhouse.[28]

"The way we have been treated is enough to make a preacher swear almost."　　　　　Union Private O.W. Norton

THE FADED COAT OF BLUE

My brave lad he sleeps in his fad-ed coat of blue, In a lone-ly grave un-known lies the heart that beat so true; He__ sank faint and hun-gry a-mong the fam-ished brave, As they laid him sad and lone-ly with-in his name-less grave.

Chorus
No more the bu-gle calls the wea-ry one, Rest nob-le spir-it in thy grave un-known! I'll find you and know you a-mong the good and true, When a robe of white is giv'n for the fad-ed coat of blue.

He cried, "Give me water and just a little crumb,
And my mother she will bless you through all the years to come;
Oh! tell my sweet sister, so gentle good and true,
That I'll meet her up in heaven in my faded coat of blue." (Chorus)

He said, "My dear comrades, you cannot take me home,
But you'll mark my grave for mother, she'll find me if she'll come;
I fear she'll not know me, among the good and true,
When I meet her up in heaven in my faded coat of blue." (Chorus)

Long, long years have vanished, and though he comes no more,
Yet my heart with startling beats with each footfall at my door;
I gaze over the hill where he waved a last adieu,
But no gallant lad I see in his faded coat of blue. (Chorus)

No sweet voice was there, breathing soft a mother's prayer,
But there's One who takes the brave and true in tender care;
No stone marks the sod o'er my lad so brave and true,
In his lonely grave he sleeps in his faded coat of blue. (Chorus)

"What's the use of killing Yankees? You kill one and six
appear in his place."   Confederate soldier

GOOBER PEAS

oward the end of the war, food was as scarce to Confederate soldiers as a hiccup at a prayer meeting. While most Southern soldiers had very little else, they did keep their sense of humor. Take, for instance, this bit of dialog between a Sergeant and a Private:

"I was eating a piece of hardtack this morning, and I bit into something soft," said a Sergeant. "A worm?" asked a Private. "No, by God, it was a ten-penny nail!"

Another soldier complained that "The only meat we had for weeks was in the biscuits." Even Yankees experienced short rations. One Hoosier soldier in Chattanooga complained in October 22, 1863 that he had lived on "two meals per day and one cracker for each meal."[24]

For Georgia soldiers, who were known as "goober grabbers," rations often came in the form of good old Georgia peanuts. "Goober Peas," although not published until 1866, was certainly among the most popular humorous songs of that era. The words were reportedly written by "A. Pindar, Esq." and music by "P. Nutt, Esq." It was actually written and published by A.E. Blackmar of New Orleans, Louisiana.

A.E. Blackmar

Who's the Jackass?

A recruiting officer stopped at a house and asked an old lady the number of males living there. After telling him the names of her husband and sons, the officer persisted and asked if there were any other males. *"Only Billy Bray,"* she answered. *"And where might he be?"* asked the officer. *"He might be in the barn,"* answered the old lady. Not finding him, the officer registered him for the draft. When his draftee failed to report for duty, the officer investigated, only to discover Billy Gray was a jackass![39]

GOOBER PEAS

Sit-ting by the road-side on a sum-mer's day, Chat-ting with my mess-mates, pass-ing time a-way, Ly-ing in the sha-dow un-der-neath the trees,

Good-ness how de-li-cious, eat-ing goo-ber peas! Peas! Peas! Peas! Peas! Eat-ing goo-ber peas! Good-ness how de-li-cious, eat-ing goo-ber peas!

When a horseman passes, the soldiers have a rule,
To cry out at their loudest, "Mister, here's your mule!"
But another pleasure enchantinger than these,
Is wearing out your grinders, eating goober peas! (Chorus)

Just before the battle the General hears a row,
He says, "The Yanks are coming, I hear their rifles now,"
He turns around in wonder, and what do you think he sees?
The Georgia Militia, eating goober peas! (Chorus)

I think my song has lasted almost long enough,
The subject's interesting, but rhymes are mighty rough,
I wish this war was over, when free from rags and fleas,
We'd kiss our wives and sweethearts and gobble goober peas! (Chorus)

N.C. Archives & History

"Breakfast! I've lived for two days now on an old boot, and a darn poor boot at that!"[39]   Confederate soldier

HARD CRACKERS COME AGAIN NO MORE

Stephen Foster

Even while professional songsmiths labored to keep up with the demand for new Civil War songs, soldiers themselves were often reworking older songs to reflect both their sorrows and their joys. Among the more humorous examples of soldiers' handiwork was "Hard Crackers Come Again No More," which was a take-off on Stephen Foster's 1855 composition, "Hard Times Come Again No More." As the most important songwriter of the age, Foster based his own composition on several Black spirituals he had heard as a boy when he accompanied his family's nurse, Olivia Pise, to church. In his last tragic days, Foster could often be found in a local barroom singing "Hard Times Come Again No More" to the appreciative, if intoxicated, clientele.[38]

Known as the "musical bellyache" of the Army of the Potomac,[3] "Hard Crackers Come Again No More" apparently originated in 1861 with the 1st Iowa Regiment. After hearing the song, their commander ordered that cornmeal mush replace crackers in the mess tent. Soon growing tired of mush, the soldiers began singing "Hard Crackers, Come Again Once More."[35]

Authentic "Cracker Lore"

- "The only meat we had for weeks was in the biscuits."
- One soldier carved a violin bridge out of a cracker.
- Union crackers were known as "Lincoln Pies," "Weevil fodder," or "McClellan Pies."
- Soldiers on both sides called crackers "teeth dullers," "sheet-iron crackers," "floor tiles," and "worm castles."
- One group of artillerists used crackers as paving stones in front of their tent.
- Solders often softened up crackers with the butt of their rifles.
- "We live on crackers so hard that if we had loaded our guns with them we could have killed Seceshs in a hurry."[28]

HARD CRACKERS COME AGAIN NO MORE

Let us close our game of pok-er, take our tin cups in hand, While we gath-er 'round the cook's tent door, Where dry mum-mies of hard crack-ers are gi-ven to each man; Oh, hard crack-ers come a-gain no more! 'Tis the song and the sigh of the hun-gry, Hard crack-ers, hard crackers, come a-gain no more! Ma-ny days you have lingered up-on our stom-achs sore, Oh, hard crack-ers, come a-gain no more.

There's a hungry, thirsty soldier, who wears his life away,
With torn clothes, whose better days are o'er;
He is sighing now for whiskey, and with throat as dry as hay,
Sings, "Hard crackers come again no more." (Chorus)

'Tis the song that is uttered in camp by night and day,
'Tis the wail that is mingled with each snore;
'Tis the sighing of the soul for spring chickens far away,
"Oh, hard crackers come again no more." (Chorus)

Recipe for Hell-Fire Stew

Boil biscuits in water until soft. Add bacon grease to taste (if available).

Chicago Historical Society

I'm so hungry I "could eat a rider off his horse...
and snap at the stirrups." Federal soldier at Chattanooga[40]

J.E.B. STUART

I t would be difficult, if not impossible, to find a Civil War soldier who loved music more than Confederate Major General J.E.B. Stuart. Even in the heat of battle, with shells bursting around him and mini balls whistling by his head, Stuart frequently sang, hummed or whistled. He was the only officer known to have his own banjo player, Sam Sweeney, who constantly serenaded him while in camp or on march. Stuart even named his horse "My Maryland,"[41]

J.E.B. Stuart

"Send me the words of 'When the Swallows & The Dew is on the Blossom,' 'Passing Away' & 'Napolitain.' Those songs which so much remind me of you." Letter to his wife from J.E.B. Stuart, Demember 12, 1861[41]

J.E.B. Stuart's Favorite Songs
"Jine the Cavalry," "Sweet Evelina," "Old Folks at Home," "When This Cruel War is Over," "Love Not," "Passing Away," "Soldier's Joy," "The Dew Is on the Blossom," "The Soldier's Dream," The Cottage by the Sea," "When the Swallows Homeward Fly," "Annie Laurie," "Lorena," "Her Bright Smile Haunts Me Still," "Ever of Thee," "Home Sweet Home," "Kathleen Mavoureen," "Passing Away,"Rock of Ages," "Napolitaine," "My Maryland."[41]

A small boy was leading a mule past an army camp. To have a little fun, one of the soldiers called out, *"Why are you holding your brother so tight, sonny?"* *"So he won't join the army,"* replied the boy.

HERE'S YOUR MULE

mong the most colorful soldiers, North or South, to inspire songsmiths to commit lyrics to paper, was John Hunt Morgan. His daring raids as a Confederate cavalry officer struck terror in the hearts of citizens living in Kentucky, Ohio and Indiana.

Bitterly disappointed when Kentucky aligned itself with the Union, Morgan and about 200 followers stole U.S. army rifles and horses and joined the Confederacy. Enlisting as a scout, he eventually rose to the rank of Brigadier General. His men, who ranged in numbers from 860 to over 5,000, were adept at living off the land by foraging. This meant that every chicken, steer, pig and ear of corn in their path was fair game and would soon become "provisions" for their roving band of marauding guerrillas. Out of these foraging expeditions came the oft-repeated praise, "Here's Your Mule." Foot soldiers found mischievous pleasure in taunting those on horseback with this expression, which became the equivalent to World War II's "Kilroy was here."

A popular and dashing figure to the Confederacy, Morgan was widely referred to as "Our Morgan" and "The Thunderbolt of the Confederacy." To the Union, he was "The Great Guerilla," The Great Freebooter" and "The King of Horse Thieves."[2] One of his favorite antics was to capture Union telegraph offices from which he communicated misleading dispatches designed to create havoc among the Federals.

With about 2,600 men, Morgan disobeyed direct orders by crossing the Ohio River in the summer of 1862 and invaded Ohio and Indiana. Though actually outnumbered by Federal troops, he skillfully gave the impression of superior numbers while the advance of his men created sheer panic among local citizens. When he was finally captured near the Pennsylvania border on July 26, 1862, it was the northernmost point reached by any armed Confederate force during the war.[2]

> *"Our 'grub' is enough to make a mule desert and a hog wish he had never been born."*   **An Illinois Corporal, October 26, 1862**

HERE'S YOUR MULE

lamming the prison door on John Hunt Morgan was easier than keeping it closed. On November 27, 1863 he escaped from the penitentiary at Columbus, Ohio by tunneling though the stone floor of his prison cell, across an open yard, and under the outside walls.[2] Although it has been said that this daring escape was the incident that inspired the creation of "Here's Your Mule,"[14] the first version of the song, "Here's Your Mule Gallop," was actually published in Nashville in 1861 by C.D. Benson as composed by Charles Stein.[32] The following year the same publisher came out with "Here's Your Mule," which was described as a "Comic Camp Song and Chorus." 1862 also saw the publication of "Here's Your Mule Schottish," composed by E. Heinemann, New Orleans, and published by P.P. Werlein & Haisey.[32] Other songs about Morgan included "How Are You, John Morgan?," "Three Cheers for Our Jack Morgan." and "John Morgan's Escape" by A.E.A. Muse.

A farm - er came to camp one day, With milk and eggs to sell, Up - on a mule that oft would stray To where no one could tell. The farm-er tir - ed of his tramp, For hours was made a fool, By ev - 'ry one he met in camp With, "Mis - ter, here's your mule." Come

Chorus
on, come on, come on old man, And don't be made a fool, By ev - 'ry - one you meet in camp With, "Mis - ter, here's your mule."

HERE'S YOUR MULE

His eggs and chickens all gone,
Before the break of day;
The "Mule" was heard of all along,
That's what the soldiers say;
And still he hunted all day long,
Alas! the witless tool,
Whilst ev'ry man would sing the song
Of, "Mister, here's your Mule." (Chorus)

John Hunt Morgan

The soldiers run in laughing mood,
Of mischief were intent;
They lifted "Muley" on their back,
Around from tent to tent;
Thro' this hole, and that, they push'd
His head and made a rule,
To shout with humorous voices all
"I say: "Mister, here's your Mule." (Chorus)

Alas! one day the mule was miss'd!
Ah! who could tell his fate?
The Farmer, like a man bereft,
Search'd early and searched late,
And as he pass'd from camp to camp,
With stricken face-the fool,
Cried out to ev'ry one he met,
Oh! "Mister, where's my Mule?" (Chorus)

"I have seen quite enough of a soldiers Life to satisfy me that it is not what it is cracked up to be."[9]

41

HOME! SWEET HOME!

ar from home and loved ones, it is not surprising that the all-time favorite song of soldiers on both sides was "Home! Sweet Home!" Ironically, of the two men who composed it, one was homeless and the other was known as a "home-wrecker." The lyrics of "Home! Sweet Home!" were written by John Howard Payne, who was born in New York City, but migrated to London seeking fame and fortune as an actor and playwright. He composed "Home! Sweet Home!" for the opera "Clari" or "The Maid of Milan." It was first produced on May 8, 1823 and it went on to become the most popular song of the entire 19th century. Although his fame was assured, financial security escaped Payne, who later served time in a debtor's prison. He was awarded the post of American consul at Tunis by President Tyler in 1842, but always lamented the fact that he never had a home.

The melody of "Home! Sweet Home!" was composed by Sir Henry Rowley Bishop, a well-known English conductor and composer of over one hundred musical works. He was known as "a noted reprobate, home-wrecker and spendthrift; and he died in poverty."[33]

For Civil War soldiers, "Home! Sweet Home!" was a potent reminder of what they had left behind. Fearing mass desertions in the Union army during the winter of 1862-63, orders were given forbidding Federal bands from playing "Home! Sweet Home!" and "Auld Lang Syne."[28]

> "The Major is a hell of a man...he dont no enough to learn a dog to bark."
> Union soldier.[13]

HOME! SWEET HOME!

'Mid__ plea - sures and pa - lac - es through__ we may roam, Be it
ev__ - er so hum - ble, there's no__ place like home; A
charm__ from the skies seems to hal__ - low us there, Which
seek__ thro' the world, is ne'er met__ with else - where.
Home! Home! sweet, sweet Home! There's
no__ place like Home!__ There's no__ place like Home!

An exile from home, splendor dazzles in vain,
Oh! give me my lowly thatched cottage again;
The birds singing gaily that came at my call;
Give me them, with the peace of mind, dearer than all. (Chorus)

To thee, I'll return, overburdened with care,
The heart's dearest solace will smile on me there.
No more from that cottage again will I roam,
Be it ever so humble, there's no place like home." (Chorus)

The Worst Music of the Civil War

The worst music of the war no doubt came from the band of the 6th Wisconsin. Soldiers were punished for misdemeanors by being assigned to the band and forced to play only one tune, "The Village Quickstep." While torturing the air with their discordant noise, they once performed for General George B. McClellan. As the band passed, the General waved, which so unglued the drum major that he stumbled, dropping his baton in the mud.[28]

JUST BEFORE THE BATTLE, MOTHER

The 19th century was the era of utter sentimentality. Songsmiths capitalized on the public's longing for songs which tugged at their tenderest heartstrings by laboring to squeeze every last drop of pathos into their songs. It was an unsuccessful performer who failed to reduce his audience to tears with a heart-felt rendition of a sentimental aire. The Civil War provided songwriters with the ultimate opportunity for sharpening their craft of creating sentimental ballads. Both for soldiers far away from home and for those who stayed behind, these sentimental songs expressed emotions deeply felt.

Though better known for his stirring patriotic songs like "The Battle Cry of Freedom," George F. Root was a master at writing sentimental ballads. In his 1891 autobiography, he tells:

"I wrote what I thought would then express the emotions of the soldiers or the people. Picturing the condition and thoughts of the soldier on the eve of an engagement, I wrote "Just Before the Battle, Mother."[16]

Library of Congress

"Just Before the Battle, Mother" was published by Root & Cady in 1862 in Chicago and went on to become one of the most popular sentimental songs of the war. It was sung by soldiers on both sides, without changing the lyrics. A Southern version was published in Richmond, Virginia by J.W. Davies & Sons ca. 1865.

JUST BEFORE THE BATTLE, MOTHER

"I clearly remember how the boys in the Thirty-third Wisconsin Infantry used to sing ['Just Before the Battle, Mother'] with almost ineffable emotion. In the dullness of camp life and on long and weary marches, it appeared to exert a helpful influence that no other song could. The words and music blended so well...in days when many a boy in peril felt all the sentiments the song expressed, that it became one of the great songs of the army."[19]

Just be-fore the bat-tle, Moth-er, I am think-ing most of you,
While up-on the field we're watch-ing, With the en-e-my in view.
Com-rades brave are 'round me ly-ing, Filled with tho'ts of home and God; For
well they know that on the mor-row Some will sleep be-neath the sod.

Chorus

Fare-well, Moth-er, you may nev-er Press me to your breast a-gain; But
oh, you'll not for-get me, Moth-er, If I'm num-bered with the slain.

Oh, I long to see you, Mother,
And the loving ones at home,
But I'll never leave our banner,
Till in honor I can come.
Tell the traitors all around you,
That their cruel words we know,
In every battle kill our soldiers
By the help they give the foe.

Hark! I hear the bugles sounding,
'Tis the signal for the fight,
Now, may God protect us, Mother,
As He ever does the right.
Here the "Battle-Cry of Freedom"
How it swells upon the air,
Oh yes, we'll rally round the standard,
Or we'll perish nobly there.

JUST BEFORE THE BATTLE, MOTHER

O n the eve of the battle at Franklin, Tennessee, November 30, 1864, a Colonel from Indianapolis was in the parlor of a nearby house. He requested the two daughters of the house to sing and play "Just Before the Battle, Mother," on the piano. Just as they began, a shell exploded within fifty yards of the house. The Colonel sprang to his feet, and ran in the direction of his regiment, but before he reached it, he was shot by a bullet which passed through him. He was taken to Nashville where he eventually recovered from his wounds. In April, four months after being shot, with the war over, he came back to Franklin expressly to get the young ladies to finish the song. His wife and more than a dozen officers accompanied him. He found the young women and they sang and played the piece through for him in the presence of all the officers, and they wept like children.[19]

Civil War MOTHER Songs

"Who Will Care For Mother Now," "Tell Mother I Die Happy," "Mother Kissed Me in My Dream," "It Was My Mother's Voice," "Shall I Never See My Mother?," "Mother Would Comfort Me," "Oh, Will My Mother Never Come?" "Dear Mother, I'm Wounded," "Mother, When the War is Over," "Mother, I'll Come Home Tonight," "Break It Gently to My Mother," "It's Growing Very Dark, Mother," "Is It Mother's Gentle Touch?" "Bear It Gently to My Mother," "The Conscript's Mother," "Dear Mother, I've Come Home to Die," "Let Me Kiss Him for His Mother," "Write a Letter to My Mother."[1]

LORENA

The sentimental song most beloved by Southern soldiers was "Lorena." It was actually written in 1857, long before the war tore soldiers from their wives and sweethearts. With little else to comfort them, "Lorena" reminded them of the separation they endured through the war's long years.

The story behind the song goes back to Massachusetts in May of 1849, when a fickle Ella Blocksom broke off her engagement with a struggling Universalist preacher named Rev. Henry De Lafayette Webster (1824-1896) in favor of a well-to-do lawyer who would later become chief justice in Ohio. Still pining after a hundred months, Webster poured out his heart in a poem written in 1857. To protect her identity, he chose the name "Lorena," based on "Lost Lenore" which he found in the writings of Edgar Allen Poe. The melody was composed by Joseph Philbrick Webster (1819-1875), who wrote the music to "In the Sweet Bye and Bye" in 1868. Scholars disagree whether or not the two Websters were brothers.

It is ironic that the most cherished love song of Confederate soldiers was written by a Northerner and first published in Chicago in 1857. Reprinted in at least nine different pirated editions in the South, virtually every pocket songster carried by Southern soldiers included "Lorena." Countless diaries and recollections of Southern soldiers mentioned that "Lorena" was by far the very favorite of the "heart" songs, closely followed by "The Girl I Left Behind Me." Even Northern soldiers sang "Lorena." The song was so popular, in fact, that countless Southern baby girls were named "Lorena" and at least two pioneer settlements and a steamship were named after her. It has been called the "Annie Laurie" of the Confederate trenches.[29] Writing in 1894, one writer said it best, "This doleful old ditty started at the start and never stopped until the last musket was stacked and the last camp fire cold."[30]

Some have even gone so far as to blame the loss of the war on "Lorena." So many Southern soldiers grew homesick and deserted after singing it, that several Generals prohibited the singing of "Lorena," but most soldiers sang it anyway.

The years creep slow-ly by, Lo-re-na, The snow is on the grass a-gain; The

sun's low down the sky, Lo-re-na, The frost gleams where the flow'rs have been. But the

heart throbs on as warm-ly now, As when the sum-mer days were nigh; Oh! the

sun can nev-er dip so low, A-down af-fec-tion's cloud-less sky.

Shoot Me!

Abraham Lincoln was surprised one day when a man drew a revolver and thrust the weapon in his face. *"What seems to be the matter?"* inquired Lincoln, with all the calmness he could muster. *"Well,"* replied the stranger, *"I swore an oath that if I ever came across an uglier man than myself I'd shoot him on the spot."*

A feeling of relief took possession of Lincoln at hearing this. *"Shoot me,"* he said to the stranger, *"for if I am an uglier man than you, I don't want to live."*[48]

Blim, Blam

"I thought they were all shooting at me. Yes sir, I thought every man in the other army was aiming at me in particular, and only me. And it seemed so darned unreasonable, you know. I wanted to explain to 'em what an almighty good fellow I was, because I thought then they might quit trying to hit me. But I couldn't explain, and they kept on being unreasonable - blim! - blam! bang! So I run!"
Stephen Crane, "The Veteran"

LORENA

We loved each other then, Lorena,
More than we ever dared to tell;
And what we might have been, Lorena,
Had but our lovings prospered well.
  But then, 'tis past, the years are gone,
  I'll not call up their shadowy forms;
  I'll say to them, "Lost years, sleep on!
  Sleep on! nor heed life's pelting storms.

The story of that past, Lorena,
Alas! I care not to repeat,
The hopes that could not last, Lorena,
They lived, but only lived to cheat.
  I would not cause e'en one regret
  To rankle in your bosom now
  For "if we *try*, we may forget,"
  Were words of thine long years ago.

Florida State Archives

Yes, these were words of thine, Lorena,
They burn within my memory yet;
They touched some tender chords, Lorena,
Which thrill and tremble with regret.
  'Twas not thy woman's heart that spoke;
  Thy heart was always true to me:
  A duty, stern and pressing, broke
  The tie which linked my soul with thee.

It matters little now, Lorena,
The past is in the eternal past;
Our heads will soon lie low, Lorena,
Life's tide is ebbing out so fast.
  There is a Future! O, thank God,
  Of life this is so small a part!
  'Tis dust to dust beneath the sod;
  But there, *up there*, 'tis heart to heart.

One Hole

"In this army one hole in the seat of the breeches indicates a Captain, two holes a Lieutenant, and the seat of the pants all out indicated the individual is a Private."   **Confederate soldier, Atlanta, June 1864.**[40]

MARCHING THROUGH GEORGIA

Sometimes a single event can leave its mark forever. Henry Clay Work was only nine years old when there occurred a tragic incident that would shape his own life and help to alter the course of 19th century music. The year was 1841, and his father, Alanson Work, was sent to prison for giving aid to several run-away slaves he met while walking down a dusty road in Missouri. The imprisonment of his father instilled in the young boy strong abolitionist feelings that would later surface in three of the most important songs of the Civil War era, "Kingdom Coming, or Year of the Jubilo," "Grafted into the Army" and "Marching Through Georgia."[19]

Henry Clay Work

After serving three to four years at hard labor, Alanson Work was released from prison at Jefferson City, Missouri on the condition that he leave Missouri and return to his native state of Connecticut."[19] The young Henry Clay Work eventually became a typesetter, tinkerer, and inventor of a rotary engine, a knitting machine and a walking doll.[29]

But the real passion of Henry Clay Work's life was writing songs. When he was sure that he had honed his song writing skills to a fine edge, he worked up his nerve and traveled to Chicago to show his newest composition to the era's most successful songwriter, George F. Root. Writing in 1891, Root recalled their first meeting:

> "One day early in the war, a quiet and rather solemn-looking young man, poorly clad, was sent up to my room from the store with a song for me to examine. I looked at it and then at him in astonishment. It was 'Kingdom Coming,' - elegant in manuscript, full of bright, good sense and comical situations in its "darkey" dialect-the words fitting the melody almost as aptly and neatly as Gilbert fits Sullivan-the melody decidedly good and taking, and the whole exactly suited to the times."[16]

MARCHING THROUGH GEORGIA

Root gave keen insight into Work's writing style:

"Mr. Work was a slow, pains-taking writer, being from one to three weeks upon a song; but when the work was done, it was like a piece of fine mosaic, especially in the fitting of words to music. His 'Marching Through Georgia' is more played and sung at the present time than any other song of the war...because it is *retrospective*. Other war songs were for exciting the patriotic feeling on *going in* to the war or the battle; 'Marching Through Georgia' is a glorious remembrance on coming triumphantly out, and so has been more appropriate to soldiers' [sic] and other gatherings ever since."[16]

"Marching Through Georgia" was written and published by Root & Cady in January, 1865, which was within a month of the end of Sherman's march. Because it was written so late in the war, its sales were limited.

Gen. William T. Sherman

It is simply ironic that "Marching Through Georgia," which was written to commemorate Sherman's march, was actually hated by the General himself. He was quoted as saying, "'Marching Through Georgia' persues me...that infernal tune smote upon my ear." He was, in fact, constantly bombarded by it as it followed him from one personal appearance to another both in America and even in Europe. In 1890, he appeared at the National Encampment of the Grand Army of the Republic in Boston. It was there he looked with dread from the reviewing stand and to his horror he saw some 250 bands plus hundreds of drum and fife corps pass in review, all playing "Marching Through Georgia." Finally, in disgust, Sherman announced that he would never attend another encampment until every band in the United States signed an agreement not to play "Marching Through Georgia" in his presence. It turned out to be his last encampment. The next time the song was played in his presence was at his own funeral![19]

MARCHING THROUGH GEORGIA

Bring the good old bug-le, boys! we'll sing a-noth-er song; Sing it with a spir-it that will start the world a-long Sing it as we used to sing it, fif-ty thou-sand strong, While we were march-ing through Geor-gia. "Hur-rah! Hur-rah! we bring the Jub-i-lee! Hur-rah! Hur-rah! the flag that makes you free!" So we sang the cho-rus from At-lan-ta to the sea, While we were march-ing through Geor-gia.

How the darkeys shouted when they heard the joyful sound!
How the turkeys gobbled which our commissary found!
How the sweet potatoes even started from the ground,
While we were marching through Georgia. (Chorus)

Yes, and there were Union men who wept with joyful tears,
When they saw the honor'd flag they had not seen for years;
Hardly could they be restrained from breaking forth in cheers,
While we were marching through Georgia. (Chorus)

"Sherman's dashing Yankee boys will never reach the coast!"
So the saucy rebels said, and 'twas a handsome boast,
Had they not forgot, alas! to reckon with the host,
While we were marching through Georgia. (Chorus)

So we made a thorough fare for Freedom and her train,
Sixty miles in latitude, three hundred to the main;
Treason fled before us, for resistance was in vain,
While we were marching through Georgia. (Chorus)

> *"The first thing in the morning is drill, then drill, then drill again. Then drill, drill, a little more drill. Then drill, and lastly drill. Between drills, we drill and sometimes stop to eat a little and have roll-call."*
> **Oliver Norton, 83rd Pennsylvania Infantry.** [20]

ithin two days of the surrender of Fort Sumter on April 13, 1861, Lincoln issued his call for 75,000 volunteers "to curb the rebellion." Among the Federal troops to answer his call was the Sixth Massachusetts Regiment, which started for Washington on April 18, 1861. While passing through Baltimore on the following day, an angry crowd of Southern sympathizers pelted them with paving stones. Killed in the fracas were at least four soldiers and twelve civilians plus thirty-one soldiers were wounded.

News of the violence soon reached the ears of Baltimore native James R. Randall, who was a professor at Poydras College, in Point Coupee Parish, Louisiana. Randall was especially affected by the news because the first man to fall in the melee was a good friend and college mate. That night, April 23, 1861, Randall was inspired to compose a poem he entitled "My Maryland." He then submitted it to the New Orleans *Delta*, where it was published on April 26, 1861.

Randall's poem was first sung in Baltimore to the French tune "Ma Normandie." It was then that two sisters, Jennie and Hetty Cary, adapted the poem to the tune of "Lauriger Horatius," which was based on the German folk tune "Tannenbaum, O Tannenbaum." In fitting the words to this tune, they changed Randall's refrain of "Maryland" to "Maryland, my Maryland." It was in this form that it was first published by Miller & Beacham, Baltimore in 1861 and by A.E. Blackmar & Bro., New Orleans in 1862.

The melody used for "Maryland, My Maryland," may be one of the oldest tunes known today. Musicologist Sigmund Spaeth has traced it to the drinking song, "Mihi est Propositum," which has been credited to the deacon Walter de Mapes, who lived in Oxford, England in the 12th century. By 1824 it was commonly sung as the Christmas carol, "Tannenbaum, O Tannenbaum."[18]

MARYLAND, MY MARYLAND

The des-pot's heel is on thy shore, Mar-y-land! my Mar-y-land! His
torch is at thy tem-ple door, Mar-y-land, my Mar-y-land! A-
venge the pat-ri-o-tic gore That flecked the streets of Balt-i-more, And
be the bat-tle queen of yore, Mar-y-land, my Mar-y-land!

Hark! to a wandering son's appeal!
Maryland! My Maryland!
My Mother-State! to thee I kneel,
Maryland! My Maryland!
For life and death, for woe and weal,
They peerless chivalry reveal,
And gird thy beauteous limbs with steel,
Maryland! My Maryland!

Thou wilt not cower in the dust,
Maryland! My Maryland!
Thy beaming sword shall never rust,
Maryland! My Maryland!
Remember Carrol's sacred trust,
Remember Howard's warlike thrust,
And all thy slumberers with the just,
Maryland! My Maryland!

Come! for thy shield is bright and strong,
Maryland! My Maryland!
Come! for thy dalliance, does thee wrong,
Maryland! My Maryland!
Come! to thine own heroic throng,
That stalks with Liberty along,
And give a new Key to thy song,
Maryland! My Maryland!

"To fill up the Army is like undertaking to shovel fleas."
Abraham Lincoln

MARYLAND, MY MARYLAND

Dear Mother! burst the tyrant's chain,
Maryland! My Maryland!
Virginia should not call in vain!
Maryland! My Maryland!
She meets her sisters on the plain -
"S*ic semper*" tis the proud refrain,
That baffles minions back amain,
Maryland! My Maryland!

I see the blush upon thy cheek,
Maryland! My Maryland!
But thou wast ever bravely meek,
Maryland! My Maryland!
But lo! there surges forth a shriek
From hill to hill, from creek to creek -
Potomac calls to Chesapeake,
Maryland! My Maryland!

Thou wilt not yield the vandal toll,
Maryland! My Maryland!
Thou wilt not crook to his control,
Maryland! My Maryland!
Better the fire upon thee roll,
Better the blade, the shot, the bowl,
Than crucifixion of the soul,
Maryland! My Maryland!

I hear the distant thunder-hum,
Maryland! My Maryland!
The Old Line's bugle, fife and drum,
Maryland! My Maryland!
She is not dead, nor deaf, nor dumb-
Huzza! She spurns the Northern scum!
She breathes - she burns!
She'll come! she'll come!
Maryland! My Maryland!

"I know if there is another war this chicken wont be thar when they enlist."   Joe Shields, Confederate private, July 1, 1861.[7]

O I'M A GOOD OLD REBEL

The bitterness felt by the South during Reconstruction is nowhere better expressed than in "O I'm a Good Old Rebel." First published in 1864 by the Blackmar Bros., the author's name was revealed only by the initials "J.R.T."[35] The 1866 edition credits the lyrics to Maj. Innes Randolph, a native of Virginia and member of General J.E.B. Stuart's staff. Randolph was a poet and essayist and it has been suggested that he wrote the lyrics not to reflect his own sentiments, but to reveal the depths of bitterness of Southern poor whites.[47]

R. Bishop Buckley

"O I'm a Good Old Rebel" bears the subtitle "A Chaunt to the Wild Western Melody, Joe Bowers." Credit for composing the melody of "Joe Bowers" goes to R. Bishop Buckley, whose 1851 composition, "Wait for the Wagon," was used by songwriters both North and South.

Mysteriously, "O I'm a Good Old Rebel" was "Respectfully Dedicated to the Hon. Thad. Stevens." It was Stevens, more than anyone else, who favored harsh treatment for the South during Reconstruction.

U.S. Army Military History Institute

> *"We have a lively time here. Every night fiddlers are plentiful."*
> **Confederate soldier from Kentucky.**[35]

O I'M A GOOD OLD REBEL

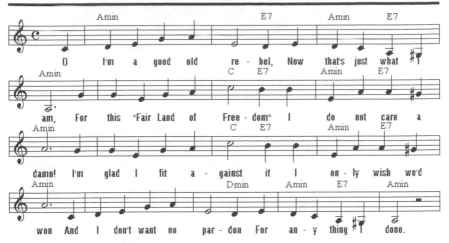

O I'm a good old re - bel, Now that's just what I
am, For this "Fair Land of Free - dom" I do not care a
damn! I'm glad I fit a - gainst it I on - ly wish we'd
won And I don't want no par - don For an - y thing done.

I hates the Constitution,
This Great Republic, too,
I hates the Freedman's Buro,
In uniforms of blue;
I hates the nasty eagle,
With all his braggs and fuss,
The lyin', thievin' Yankees,
I hates 'em wuss and wuss.

I hates the Yankee nation
And everything they do,
I hates the Declaration
Of Independence, too;
I hates the glorious Union-
'Tis dripping with our blood-
I hates their striped banner,
I fit it all I could.

I followed old mas' Robert
For four year, near about,
Got wounded in three places
And starved at Pint Lookout;
I cotch the roomatism
A campin' in the snow,
But I killed a chance o' Yankees,
I like to kill some mo'.

Three hundred thousand Yankees
Is stiff in Southern dust;
We got three hundred thousand
Before they conquered us;
They died of Southern fever
And Southern steel and shot;
I wish they was three million
Instead of what we got.

I can't take up my musket
And fight 'em now no more,
But I aint a going to love 'em,
Now that is sarten sure;
And I don't want no pardon
For what I was and am,
I won't be reconstructed
And I don't care a dam.

Battle of the Bands

In early December 1862, the Union and Confederate armies gathered on opposite sides of the Rappahannock River near Fredericksburg, Virginia to do battle. One evening a Confederate band came forward and played "Dixie." From across the river, a Union band responded with "John Brown's Body." The Confederates "retaliated" with "The Bonnie Blue Flag" and received "The Star-Spangled Banner" in return. Finally, the music ceased and silence descended over the battle arena. Then a lone Union bugler played the haunting melody of "Home! Sweet Home!" A New Hampshire soldier later wrote in his diary that "as the sweet sounds rose and fell on the evening air...all listened intently, and I don't believe there was a dry eye in all those assembled thousands."[28]

NAMES FOR THE WAR

The War for Separation
The War of the Sections
The War for Constitutional Liberty
The Confederate War
Mr. Davis' War
Mr. Lincoln's War
The Southern Rebellion
The Great Rebellion
The War for Southern Rights
The War of Northern Aggression
The Reb Time
The Late Unpleasantness
The War for Abolition
The War for Southern Liberty
The Second American Revolution
The War of Yankee Arrogance
The War of Southern Arrogance
The War of the 1860's
The War for Southern Independence
The War of Secession[12]

"I wish to God one half of our officers were knocked in the head by slinging them against a part of those still left."[40]   **Rebel soldier**

"Gentlemen, if we had your songs, we'd have whipped you out of your boots! Who wouldn't have marched or fought with such songs? We had nothing, absolutely nothing, except the bastard 'Marseillaise' and 'The Bonny Blue Flag' and 'Dixie.' which were nothing but jigs."[5]

Confederate officer after General Lee's surrender

He Fiddled Himself Out of Prison

The Captain of a Confederate prison at Camp Chase, near Columbus, Ohio surprised everyone by announcing that he was

U.S. Army Military History Institute

going to hold a fiddle contest that day and the winner would go free. Among the many great fiddlers was a prisoner named Sol Carpenter, better known as "Devil Sol." Sol's best tune was called "George Booker," although it was actually a 1780's tune entitled "The Marquis of Huntly's Farewell."[35] Afraid the tune was not quite good enough to win his freedom, Sol made up some parts to it right on the spot. After all the fiddlers had played, Sol was asked to play his tune again. When the Captain was satisfied he had found the best fiddler, he gave Sol his freedom. The tune has since been called "Camp Chase."[36]

"Our soldiers were pitching around like a blind dog in a meat hous."[40]

TENTING ON THE OLD CAMP GROUND

ven the hills of New Hampshire could not shield Walter Kittredge from the war. The night before traveling to Concord to enlist in the Union army, he could not sleep. As John Hutchinson later wrote:

"He thought of the many dear boys already gone over to the unseen shore, killed in battle or dead from disease in the camps, of the unknown graves, of the sorrowful homes; of the weary waiting for the end of the cruel strife, and the sorrow in camps, of the brave boys waiting for the coming battle, which might be their last. Suddenly...he arose and began to write."[37]

After completing the song, "Tenting on the Old Camp Ground," Kittredge traveled to Concord to enlist, but was rejected for "feebleness of constitution." Though he could not contribute to the military effort, Kittredge was determined to contribute to the war effort by performing patriotic and sentimental songs for Union soldiers. Ironically, he lived an active and healthy life and died at the ripe old age of 72.

Undaunted by the fact that "Tenting on the Old Camp Ground" was turned down for publication by a Boston publisher in 1862, Kittredge showed his composition to his friend, John Hutchinson, of the popular singing group, The Hutchinsons. After singing it at their concerts at High Rock, Massachusetts, the song was hailed with great enthusiasm. At the urging of Asa Hutchinson, Oliver Ditson Co. published the song in 1864, with copies priced at eight cents each. In the first two months after publication, 10,000 copies were sold. By the war's end sales had reached 100,000 copies. Incredibly, sales remained high through the end of the 19th century and into the early 20th century. In fact, royalties in 1898 were greater than in any previous year. No novice to the publishing business, Asa Hutchinson had dealt himself in from the beginning for half the publisher royalties, so his proceeds from "Tenting on the Old Camp Ground" far exceeded any sum he received for the songs he had written as a member of the Hutchinsons.

TENTING ON THE OLD CAMP GROUND

Despite great popularity on both sides, one New Hampshire soldier took a particular dislike to the song. "That song is especially dedicated to the brave and stalwart home-stayers while they do furious battle with the ferocious minnow, the deadly trout, the blood-thirsty angle-worm and the awe-inspiring bull-frog...along the bold and dangerous shores of New England summer mill-ponds and meadow brooks. For real soldiers all the color such songs ever had is just now washed out with an ocean of mud and water."[28]

We're tent-ing to-night on the old camp ground, Give us a song to cheer. Our wea-ry hearts, a song of home, And friends we love so dear.

Chorus

Ma-ny are the hearts that are wear-y to-night, Wish-ing for the war to cease;

Ma-ny are the hearts that are look-ing for the right To see the dawn of peace.

Tent-ing to-night, tent-ing to-night, Tent-ing on the old camp ground.

We've been tenting tonight on the old camp ground
Thinking of days gone by,
Of the loved ones at home that gave us the hand,
And the tear that said goodbye! (Chorus)

We are tired of war on the old camp ground,
Many are dead and gone,
Of the brave and true who've left their homes,
Others been wounded long. (Chorus)

We've been fighting today on the old camp ground
Many are lying near;
Some are dead and some are dying,
Many are in tears. (Chorus)

TRAMP! TRAMP! TRAMP!

hose who marched gallantly off to war never dreamed that many of them would end up in prison. But by the time "Tramp, Tramp, Tramp" was composed by George F. Root and published by Root & Cady in 1864, hundreds of thousands of Union and Confederate troops were being held as prisoners of war. Despite the horrifying conditions at infamous prisons such as Andersonville and Libby Prison, "Tramp, Tramp, Tramp" gave, in Root's own words, "a more hopeful view..."[16] Comparing how the song stacked up against his other well-known compositions, Root explained that "'Tramp' was the last successful one, and had but a short life - less than a year, but in that time our profit on it was ten thousand dollars."[16]

Further proof of its popularity was published in *The Chicago Tribune*, January 14, 1865:

"It has been sung all the week at the Academy of Music and other places of amusement, and has at times won a <u>double encore</u>, the company being compelled by the audience to sing it three times."[11]

The fame of "Tramp, Tramp, Tramp" even spilled beyond America's borders. Japanese soldiers were said to have marched to the tune of "Tramp, Tramp, Tramp," in April of 1895, with only minor rhythmic changes.[11]

"Soldiering does well for a few months, but it dont ware like *farming.*" Union volunteer

TRAMP! TRAMP! TRAMP!

In the pri-son cell I sit Think-ing Moth-er, dear, of you, And our bright and hap-py home so far a-way, And the tears they fill my eyes 'Spite of all that I can do, Tho' I try to cheer my com-rades and be gay.

Chorus

Tramp, tramp, tramp, the boys are march-ing, Cheer up, com-rades, they will come And be-neath the star-ry flag We shall breathe the air a-gain, Of the free-land in our own be-lov-ed home.

In the battle front we stood
When their fiercest charge they made,
And they swept us off, a hundred men or more,
But before we reached their lines,
They were beaten back dismayed,
And we heard the cry of victory o'er and o'er.
(Chorus)

So within the prison cell
We are waiting for the day,
That shall come to open wide the iron door,
And the hollow eyes grow bright,
And the poor heart almost gay,
As we think of seeing home and friends once more.
(Chorus)

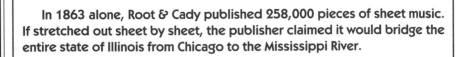

In 1863 alone, Root & Cady published 258,000 pieces of sheet music.
If stretched out sheet by sheet, the publisher claimed it would bridge the
entire state of Illinois from Chicago to the Mississippi River.

THE VACANT CHAIR

he image of an empty chair at the dinner table was a potent reminder of the many losses suffered during the war. The song was first published by Root & Cady in Chicago in 1861 with words indicated only by the initials H.S.W. and music by George F. Root. The copyright was not applied for until September 26, 1862.

The mysterious H.S.W. turned out to be 85 year old Henry S. Washburn of Worcester, Massachusetts. During Thanksgiving of 1861, he was a guest in the home of 18-year old Lieutenant John William Grout of the 15th Massachusetts Infantry, who had died only a month before at the battle of Balls Bluff, Virginia. Ironically, Grout had received a furlough and expected to be home for Thanksgiving. Instead, in the battle on October 21, 1861, he displayed true heroism by sacrificing his own life in an effort to help wounded comrades cross a river during a retreat by Federal troops under General McClellan. After bringing a boatload of wounded soldiers across the river, Grout was forced to plunge into the river to try to avert capture or death. His last words, as remembered by a fellow soldier, were "Tell Company D I could have reached the shore-but-I'm shot."[19]

At the Thanksgiving table on November 28, 1861, Henry S. Washburn was struck by Grout's empty chair and soon composed his poem, which he sent to a local newspaper, the Worcester *Spy*, for publication. Washburn's poem soon found its way to George F. Root, who created the melody and published it as "The Vacant Chair; or We Shall Meet, but We Shall Miss Him." The poignancy of the lyrics insured its popularity on both sides of the war. A number of Confederate editions were published by J.H. Hewitt of Augusta, John C. Schreiner & Son of Macon and Savannah, and Davies & Sons of Richmond.[32]

"The Vacant Chair" became a part of virtually every veteran's funeral, North and South, for many years after the war.

THE VACANT CHAIR

We shall meet, but we shall miss him, There will be one va-cant chair; We shall
lin-ger to ca-ress him While we breathe our even-ing prayer. When a
year a-go we gath-ered, Joy was in his mild blue eye, But a
gold-en chord is sev-ered, And our hopes in ru-in lie. We shall

Chorus
meet but we shall miss him, There will be one va-cant chair; We shall
lin-ger to ca-ress him, When we breathe our even-ing prayer.

At our fireside, sad and lonely,
Often will the bosom swell,
At remembrance of the story
How our noble Willie fell;
How he strove to bear our banner
Through the thickest of the fight,
And uphold our country's honor,
In the strength of manhood's might.

True they tell us wreaths of glory
Ever more will deck his brow,
But this soothes the anguish only
Sweeping o'er our heart-string now.
Sleep today, oh, early fallen,
In thy green and narrow bed,
Dirges from the pine and cypress
Mingle with the tears we shed.

Herb Peck, Jr.

> "I am well at the present with the exception I have the Dyerear and I
> hope these few lines will find you the same."
>> Letter from Federal soldier to his wife[40]

WEEPING, SAD AND LONELY

T he song that deeply touched the hearts of soldiers and home folks on both sides was "Weeping, Sad And Lonely," or, "When This Cruel War is Over." Published by Sawyer & Thompson in Brooklyn, N.Y. in 1863, the words were written by Charles Carroll Sawyer with music composed and arranged by Henry Tucker. The sheet music cover advertised it as sung by Wood's Minstrels, Broadway, N.Y. and was "Inscribed to Sorrowing Hearts At Home." The price was 25 cents.

Trying to explain his motivation for writing the song, Sawyer later wrote:

"During the year 1861-62, many songs were published, but they were all filled with the love of the soldier for those whom he had left at home, and, thinking it would cheer and comfort our brave boys, I composed and published the song, which seemed to reach the hearts of both armies, so that in a few months I found it almost impossible to supply the demand."[35]

With sales approaching one million copies, keeping up with the demand for "Weeping, Sad and Lonely" proved to be a difficult, if enviable, problem. Though the song originated in Brooklyn, N.Y., its popularity was widespread on both sides, with at least four Confederate versions including those published in Richmond, Virginia by Geo. Dunn & Co and in Columbia, South Carolina by Julian A. Selby c. 1864. In the Southern versions, minor changes were made, including the substitution of "gray" for "blue" in the first verse.

Sawyer's other songs never even came close to the popularity of "Weeping, Sad And Lonely." Some of them included: "Swing in the Lane," "Peeping Through the Bars," "Who Will Care for Mother Now?" "Mother Would Comfort Me," and the reply song, "Coming Home; or The Cruel War is Over."

So destructive of morale was "Weeping, Sad And Lonely" that several Generals forbad soldiers to sing it.

"This countrie is so por it wolden hardle sprout pees."
A Georgia soldier writing from Wilmington, N.C.[40]

WEEPING, SAD AND LONELY

Dear-est love, do you re-mem—ber, When we last did meet,
How you told me that you loved— me, Kneel-ing at my feet?
Oh! how proud you stood be-fore— me In your— suit of blue,
When you vow'd to me and coun-try Ev-er to be true.

Chorus

Weep-ing, sad and lone-ly, Hopes and fears how— vain!
When this cru-el war is o— ver, Pray-ing that we meet a - gain

When the summer breeze is sighing
Mournfully along;
Or when autumn leaves are falling,
Sadly breathes the song.
Oft in dreams I see thee lying
On the battle plain,
Lonely, wounded, even dying,
Calling, but in vain. (Chorus)

If amid the din of battle
Nobly you should fall,
Far away from those who love you,
None to hear you call.
Who would whisper words of comfort,
Who would soothe your pain?
Ah! the many cruel fancies
Even in my brain. (Chorus)

But our country called you, darling,
Angels cheer your way;
While our nation's songs are fighting,
We can only pray.
Nobly strike for God and liberty,
Let all nations see,
How we love the starry banner,
Emblem of the free. (Chorus)

Charles Carroll Sawyer

> "The officers are not fit to tote guts *to a bear.*" Confederate soldier

67

WHEN JOHNNY COMES MARCHING HOME

esides "Battle Hymn of the Republic," "When Johnny Comes Marching Home" is the Civil War song most remembered by the American people. Its triumphant melody and comforting words have given it a longevity not enjoyed by most other Civil War era compositions.

"When Johnny Comes Marching Home" was written in 1863 by Patrick S. Gilmore, the well-known bandmaster of the Union army under the pseudonym Louis Lambert. The tune was apparently adapted from an old Irish song entitled, "Johnny I Hardly Knew Ye." But even though this melody was originally composed in 1802, when Irish soldiers fought in Ceylon, it still had strong appeal to citizens on both sides of the Civil War who missed their sons, husbands and brothers.[23]

U.S. Army Military History Institute

"We have drummer boys with us that when they came at first they could hardly look you in the face for diffidence but now could stare the Devil out of contenance and can't be beat at cursing, swearing and gambling."
A. Davenport, Union soldier, December 13, 1861

One drummer boy, J.H. Kendig, sold cakes, nuts, watermelons and other treats to Northern soldiers. He was so sucessful that in a letter dated August 10, 1863, he included the sum of sixty-five dollars.[13]

"A crow flying over the valley wold have to carry his own *provisions.*" David Nichol, Union soldier, May 21, 1864.[7]

WHEN JOHNNY COMES MARCHING HOME

When John-ny comes march-ing home a-gain, Hur-rah,___ hur-rah!___ We'll give him a heart-y wel-come then, Hur-rah,___ hur-rah!___ The___ men will cheer,___ the boys will shout, The la-dies they___ will all turn out, And we'll all feel gay, When John-ny comes march-ing home.

The old church bell will peal with joy,
Hurrah, hurrah!
To welcome home our darling boy,
Hurrah, hurrah!
The village lads and lassies say
With roses they will strew the way,
And we'll all feel gay,
When Johnny comes marching home.

Get ready for the jubilee,
Hurrah, hurrah!
We'll give the hero three times three,
Hurrah, hurrah!
The laurel wreath is ready now,
To place upon his loyal brow,
And we'll all feel gay,
When Johnny comes marching home.

Let love and friendship on that day,
Hurrah, hurrah!
Their choicest treasures then display,
Hurray, hurrah!
And let each one perform some part,
To fill with joy the warrior's heart,
And we'll all feel gay,
When Johnny comes marching home.

"We have to drink wate[r] thick with mud & wigel tails."
Confederate soldier.[40]

TRUE TALES OF THE CIVIL WAR

At the battle of Shiloh or Pittsburg Landing, Colonel A. K. Johnson of the Twenty-Eighth Illinois Regiment got the surprise of his life. He tried to pull a Confederate officer from his horse by grabbing his hair, but his wig came off instead!

Unimpressed with women in a north Mississippi town, one Union soldier wrote, "[They are] sharp-nosed tobacco-chewing, snuff-spitting, flax-headed, hatchet-faced, yellow-eyed, sallow-skinned, cotton-dressed, flat-breasted, bare-headed, long-waisted, hump-shouldered, stoop-necked, big-footed, straddle-toed, sharp-shinned, thin-lipped, pale-faced, lantern-jawed, silly-looking damsels."[13]

The Origin of "Taps"

While campaigning on the Virginia peninsula, "Taps" was composed by Federal Major General Daniel Butterfield, chief of staff to General Hooker. He whistled it to his bugler, who wrote it down on the back of an envelope. Butterfield ordered that the tune would signal lights out at day's end. It was soon picked up by other buglers, and eventually became regulation.[28]

An old woman who was standing in the doorway of her log cabin was asked by Indiana volunteers, *"Well, old lady, are you a Secessionist?"* *"No,"* she answered. *"Are you a Unionist?"* *"No, I'm not."* *"Well, what are you, then?"* *"A Baptist, and always have been."*[39]

THANKS!

hanks to all who contributed to *Rousing Songs & True Tales of the Civil War*: Barbara Swell, Janet Swell, Lori & John Erbsen, Beverly Teeman, Steve Millard, Bob Willoughby, Leon Swell, Rita, Wes & Leann Erbsen, Justin Hallman, Pam Budd, Mary Brown of Warren Wilson College Library, Webb Garrison, Caroline Moseley, Dale Rose, Dave Gorski, Trace Edward Zaber, John Braden, Sherri George and Linda Sides.

The cover is "The Wounded Drummer Boy" by Eastman Johnson, 1870, courtesy of Union League Club. The illustrated capital letters were drawn before 1890 by Edwin Forbes.

Sources

1. *Songs of the Civil War* by Irwin Silber, 1960; 2. *The Singing Sixties* by Willard A. & Porter W. Heaps, 1960; 3. *Singing Soldiers* by Paul Glass, 1964; 4. *American Wit and Humor* by David Simonds, 1900; 5. *Stories of Civil War Songs* by Ernest K. Emurian 1960; 6. *Lincoln and the Music of the Civil War* by Kenneth A. Bernard, 1966; 7. *A House Divided* ed. by Edward L. Ayers and Kate Cohen, 1997; 9. *The Life of Johnny Reb* by Bell I. Wiley, 1943; 10. *The Civil War Notebook* by Albert A. Nofi, 1993; 11. *Music Publishing in Chicago Before 1871* by Dena Epstein, 1969; 12. *A Civil War Treasury* by Albert A. Nofi, 1992; 13. *The Life of Billy Yank* by Bell Irwin Wiley, 1952; 14. *Confederate Music* by Richard B. Harwell, 1950; 15. *War Songs and Poems of the Southern Confederacy* by H.M. Wharton, D.D., 1904; 16. *The Story of a Musical Life* by George F. Root, 1891; 18. *A History of Popular Music in America* by Sigmund Spaeth, 1948; 19. *Stories of Great National Songs* by Colonel Nicholas Smith, 1899; 20. *Brothers in Arms* by William C. Davis, 1995; cont...

SOURCES (CONTINUED)

23. *Folk Songs of North America* by Alan Lomas, 1960; 24. *The Civil War* ed. William C. Davis and Bell I. Wiley, 1981; 26. "Dan Emmett - The Man Who Wrote Dixie," by Wayne Erbsen, *Banjo Newsletter*, February, 1980; 27. *Stories of Civil War Songs* by Ernerst K. Emurian, 1960; 28. *Soldiers Blue and Gray* by James I. Robertson, Jr., 1988; 29. *Campfires and Battle-fields*, Rossiter Johnson, ca. 1894; 30. *Pen and Ink* by Brander Matthews, 1894; 31. *A Pictorial History of Civil War Era Musical Instruments & Military Bands* by Robert Garofalo and Mark Elrod, 1985; 32. *Confederate Sheet-Music Imprints* by Frank W. Hoogerwerf, 1984; 33. *Front Porch Songs, Jokes & Stories* by Wayne Erbsen, 1993; 35. *Civil War Music* notes by Charles K. Wolfe, 1991; 36. *The Hammons Family*, ed. by Carl Fleischhauer and Alan Jabbour, 1973; 37. *Story of the Hutchinsons* by John Wallace Hutchinson, 1896; 38. *A Treasury of Stephen Foster* by John Tasker Howard, 1946; 39. *Blue & Gray Laughing*, edited by Paul Zall, 1996; 40. *The Common Soldier of the Civil War* by Bell I. Wiley, 1973; 41. "Those Songs which So Much Remind Me of You" by Caroline Moseley, *American Music*, Winter 1991; 42. *Abe Lincoln Laughing*, ed. P.M. Zall, 1995; 44. *Civil War Wordbook* by Darryl Lyman, 1994; 47. *Collier's*, April 4, 1914, p. 20-21; 48. *A Treasury of American Anecdotes* by B.A. Botkin, 1957.

> *"The common private soldier earns enough in one month to buy a pretty fair watermelon."*
>   T.P. Forrester, Confederate soldier from Georgia, September 11, 1864.[7]